LET US PRAY

PASTOR LYDIA E. TORRES

LET US PRAY

Copyright © 2020 by Lydia E. Torres

Let Us Pray

Published in the United States of America
ISBN 978-1-7340305-8-7

All rights are reserved solely by the author. The author declares that the contents are original and do not infringe on the rights of any other person.

No part of this book may be reproduced in any form except with permission from the author.

All scripture references and quotations are taken from the Holy Bible, KJV, used by permission.

Dedication

I dedicate this book to my husband of twenty-six years, Christopher Torres, a man who has encouraged my gifts, career, and has never been afraid of God's anointing on my life. We have experienced great successes and have also been through pain but through all that God has preserved our love for each other.

I dedicate this book to both of my sons, Christopher L. and Xavier S. Torres who have witnessed great miracles and blessings from God. They have been a source of great joy and I look forward to all that God has promised them.

I dedicate this book to my dad who I lost fourteen years ago. I miss him greatly, but I know He is in the hands of God enjoying His presence and promises.

Lastly, I dedicate this book to all the men and women who are struggling in developing a prayer life that is impactful and brings about the results they are longing for. Don't give up continue to pray through.

Reflection

Rev. Lydia Torres speaks and lives with profound authority in the area of prayer and spiritual intimacy. Her entire life with God commends her credibility and seasoned experience in this all-important territory. She is most divinely gifted to know God and make Him known. If you want to pray effectively and successfully, listen to everything she says and apply it, I do!

Rev. John Chandler Cleveland

Table of Contents

Chapter	Page
Prologue	6
What is Prayer	8
The Hebrew Perspective on Prayer	10
What Does the Bible tell us about our duty to pray?	13
What is it Then to Pray?	20
To Pray is To?	22
To Pray is Not	26
Preparing Yourself to Pray	34
Examining the Lord's Prayer /Praying to God	42
As Promised Constant and Consistency	46
Praying: Why Do It at All?	48

LET US PRAY

**Types of Prayers/Prayer Can
Take on Many Forms**……………………………..53

Summary……………………………………………..68

The Prayer Appendix…………………………..70

Epilogue……………………………………………86

Thank You…………………………………………88

About the Author……………………………….89

Prologue

God regularly uses his daughters for mighty tasks. When the Book of the Law was found during the reign of King Josiah, it was the prophetess Huldah who was consulted to confirm its authenticity. Often overlooked is the fact that Josiah could have consulted the prophets Jeremiah, Zephaniah, or Habbakuk, but did not. Hundreds of years later, when Paul closed his letter to the Church in Rome, he made sure to acknowledge the servants involved in the early formation of the universal church-such as Phoebe, a minister, Prisca, a missionary, and Junia, an apostle described as "outstanding among the apostles." Those who are wise, humble, contrite and Spirit-led do not diminish God's use of such women.

We would treat our sisters as less than equal heirs to the promise of God's covenant relationship if we foolishly discounted their value to Him and their power to be used by Him. We would certainly make that mistake if we discounted the work we are holding in our hands.

While I am honored to, in a sense, introduce this work, I am also blessed by it. The author is my wife of more than 32 years, and me are direct beneficiaries of this praying wife and mother.

Others in Lydia's life are direct beneficiaries of a praying pastor, teacher, mentor, and friend. It is people like Pastor Lydia whom we all need in our lives.

LET US PRAY

Pastor Lydia's work represents spiritual insight and practical advice based on years of studying the purpose and power of prayer as enlightened in Scripture. She does so effortlessly because it comes from one who practices what she preaches. Pastor Lydia has been committed to spending meaningful time in daily prayer long before I knew her and in all the time since. Consequently, in addition to studying prayer, she writes from what has become a rare perspective of daily devotional practice.

Pastor Lydia is uniquely focused on God's will in her life and the lives of others. And when it comes to prayer, she speaks from commitment and experience. If one hopes to recognize a Christian who is truly devoted to prayer look at their knees, listen to their words, and feel for their hearts. In Pastor Lydia, one will see, hear, and discern the evidence of a prayerful life. Anyone who lives a life enriched by regular prayer will recognize this immediately and find confirmation in this work and those who do not, will learn much from it.

If you have the opportunity to read and study Lydia's work, it may be that somewhere, somehow, and at some time someone prayed for you. If not, this may be a wonderful moment of God's divine intervention in your life. Either way, enjoy God's grace and blessings for all they are, which is immeasurable. As you will find, this book is about praying it forward to glorify God, thanking Him for His amazing grace, being a blessing in the lives of others, and finding peace in your private time with the God who created it all.

Chris Torres - Loving Husband

What is Prayer?

In order to understand why God calls us to pray, we must first understand what prayer is. Since the bible was first written in Aramaic, Hebrew and Greek it makes sense to look at the word prayer from its own beginning.

The Hebrew word for prayer is the word *Telfilah.* The word Telfilah comes from another word *Pellel* that means to judge. The word *Pellel* has a root word *Pal* or Palal meaning to fall. The root word *Pal* is the root word for fall. The word "fall" etymologically is written as *Phalpal*. The word *Phalpal* is also the root word for *naphal* also meaning to fall. So, in looking at the entire origin of the word we find that the total meaning of prayer is this; to fall down or bow down to the ground prostrate before a sovereign authority to plead one's cause. We can read an example of this in Is. 45:14 where the Sabeans fall down and make supplications to Cyrus the King.

LET US PRAY

Let's look again at the word *Telfilah*. The word *Telfilah* which comes from the root word *Pellel* or *Hitpallel* means to judge, to self-reflect, self-evaluate and to become introspective. *Telfilah* is a time to go into one's self to see what one needs, to examine what one is all about. To determine one's faults and qualities so that one can determine what is needed from God and why God should give it to us. *Telfilah* also means attachment. When we pray, we become attached or one with God so that the flesh no longer separates us from God. This connection is a spiritual connection. Prayer allows our spirit man to become attached to God, which then allows for our spirit man to take over. This connection creates a powerful atmosphere where the Holy Spirit can pray through us.

Not surprising, the Yiddish word for prayer is *Daven,* from which we get the word divine. The word Daven simply means to move one's lips together or to bring one's lips together. This act of Daven means to bring together two things to become one. When we *Daven* we create a bond between God and us. Prayer then is the act of bringing God and man together.

To pray is to bow down before a sovereign ruler in authority; to make supplications, before him as to your needs, failings, and desires. In doing so, we create a bond between God and us.

The Hebrew Perspective on Praying

Scientists believe that men have been praying or participating in some form of prayer (meditation) as far back as five thousand years. The children of God in the Old Testament knew how to pray when they needed God to set them free and destroy their enemies. The Orthodox Jew is still instructed in the art of praying. Their way of presenting themselves before God has remained largely unchanged.

As we stated earlier, prayer is *Telfilah*; the process of uniting ourselves back to God. It is through prayer that we raise ourselves above the whole succession of life that prevails during the rest of the day. In Jewish culture prayer has two purposes:
1. To increase your awareness of God in your life and to increase the role that God plays in your life.
2. Practice humility. When we pray, we are practicing a type of humility before God.

This type of spiritual humility only comes through prayer.

In Jewish culture the example of this unification and awareness of God is seen in the story of Jacob's Ladder. Jacob's Ladder is the unification of man to heaven and to God. Prayer is the ladder that brings access to God back to man and vice versa.

Jewish prayer time is broken up into four stages:

1. **Praising**: all adoration is given to God. The person spends time giving God praise for everything in their life that God has done, provided or given. This time is seen as an opportunity to express gratitude to God for all He has done. Joshua 23:15a "therefore it shall come to pass, that as all good things are come upon you, which the Lord your God promised you.
2. **Blessing**: In this stage the person spends time blessing the name of God. It is here where we acknowledge Him for all He is and for all His characteristics. For example, His love, His patience, His peace, His power and His wisdom. During this time God is hailed as the savior, healer, liberator, protector and provider. This is the time when God's greatness is exalted.
3. **Needs**: In this prayer segment the individual needs are revealed to God. This is the time where the need for help, guidance, finances, direction and other necessities are brought before God. In doing this, God is acknowledged as the only one who can provide and supply for all present and future needs.

LET US PRAY

4. **His Will be Done on Earth as it is in Heaven**: This last stage of prayer is reserved for the asking of God to exercise His will on earth as it is done ~~so~~ in heaven. There's no doubt as to who is in command in heaven since God is the ultimate authority. "The earth is the Lord's and the fullness thereof and all who live in it. (Ps. 24:1) but the devil who is the prince of darkness wields demonic influences over people and the decisions they make. Praying God's will be done on earth is to pray God's influence be the only influence in man's life, as in heaven.

These stages in Jewish prayer are often referred to as Jacob's Ladder. Each stage of prayer is seen as a rung on the ladder leading them closer and closer to a more intimate communion during their prayer time. So Jacobs Ladder was not just a sign to Jacob but it has also served as a vehicle of progressive access to God.

What Does the Bible Tell Us About Our Duty to Pray?

God expects us to pray continually and to not faint in our devotion to prayer. (Col. 4:2, Luke 18:1). Praying takes dedication and discipline. The same discipline we may give our favorite program, our job and even our children is the same discipline that is required in prayer. I sometimes think that people believe that prayer requires a different devotion than what we give to other things we draw pleasure from. The things we enjoy or care about are the things we are committed to. Prayer requires commitment. Commitment in prayer is really fidelity or faithfulness. We are faithful to what and whom we choose. I have heard people say to me "I can't pray because I don't feel like praying." I don't always feel like praying either, but I have found that when I pray despite how I feel, God is faithful and gives me strength to overcome those feelings so I can pray. When we stay away from God's presence, we lose interest in

LET US PRAY

Him and we demonstrate a lack of faithfulness towards God. We can claim to love God all we want to, but would we trust someone who claimed they loved us but never spoke to us! I dare say, I do not believe that that relationship or friendship would last for very long. We as humans need contact with those we care about. If we love God, then we should make contact with Him every day.

The scriptures tell us that we must "pray without ceasing" (I Thess. 5:17). The word ceasing in the Hebrew has many meanings much like the English word itself. The word for ceasing in Hebrew is *Chadal*. This word means to leave undone, forbear, deserted, fail, hold back, let alone, neglect, quit and refrain. When we don't pray, we are deserting our post, we are holding back from God, we are neglecting our responsibility to Him. We are to constantly remain prayerful. We tend to separate parts of our lives out into sections, but God sees our life as one continuous motion. Prayer doesn't have to be reserved for church times. It can happen all day long.

Our duty is to watch and pray (Luke 21:36). When we pray, we are not to ignore what is going on around us spiritually. We must be sober and vigilant (I Peter 5:8), knowing full well that the enemy is lurking around looking to devour us. So, when we pray, we pray in an alert manner. The enemy should never catch us off guard. His schemes have been the same for thousands of years. The enemy waits for the time when we are most vulnerable to attack, confuse, depress and deceive. Let's be watchful always.

Prayer is where our dedication to God is tested. As stated before, prayer requires dedication and discipline from us. God will always allow us to be tried in the area where we are in greatest need of growth. How does God get us to pray? He sends in a trial. Have you not noticed that when we are going through something difficult this is when we find ourselves pushing into God via our prayer life? If this is the only time God can get you to go to your knees repeatedly, then God will allow difficult times to visit repeatedly. To be tried is biblical. The word tells us that in this world we would have afflictions (John 16:33), but that we would overcome. However, we all know people who seem to be caught in a never-ending cycle of problems. Could it be that this is the only way God can get them to pray? To be tried is God's way of knowing what we are made of. Are we gold, silver, iron, wood or hay? I Peter 1:7 and Job 23:10 tell us about the testing of the vessel to see if it can withstand the fire. Being placed in the fire from time to time is God's will but being kept in the fire is sometimes our doing. Get on your knees so He can get you out of the fire!

Prayer is where our purpose is really determined. As we pray and remain committed in prayer, God begins to unfold His purpose in us. God has a plan for all His children. However, God, in His infinite wisdom, will not allow us full access to our purpose until we have established a firm foundation in Him. This firm foundation is built on a life that is given to the Lord. When my brother was 13 he asked God to teach him how to play the Bass Guitar. He could not read music, nor had he ever taken a lesson. My dad bought him a Bass, a small amplifier and some music books in support of the desire he expressed. I watched my brother at

LET US PRAY

first struggle to teach himself how to play until one day he put the books away. He told us he was going too fast and pray for three days so that God would teach him. He spent the whole weekend in his room praying and fasting. Then on the very last night I started to hear a melody coming from his room. He was actually playing. God gave him a song (Open Thou My Eyes). From that day until now, my brother is an extremely talented Bass Guitarist that still does not read music. The music he hears comes from the Lord. Our purpose, gifts and even future talents are wrapped up in our prayer life. God wants all that He has intended for our lives to come to pass. We are God's children and He loves us. What won't God do for us if we pray? God's word reminds us that if we pray, He will hear our prayers, forgive our sin and heal our land (II Chronicles 7:14). This phrase "heal our land" means spiritual healing, physical healing and overall wellness. This phrase also means to be restored back to a time of fullness, growth and production. Let God release and restore your purpose in Him.

We either maintain communion with God or we don't. When we pray, we are participating in a deep communion with God. We are communing with God. Praying allows us to express our hopes, desires and dreams before God but it also draws us into His presence. When we enter into God's presence via prayer, we are exposed to all of God's grace, love, mercy and peace. This union in prayer creates an atmosphere where God can speak to us. Prayer is not just about what we have to say to but it is also about what He has to say to us. It is in God's presence that we can experience fullness of joy (Ps. 16:11). In prayer we enter God's presence where we can experience Him and know Him face to face (I Cor. 13:12). It is in prayer that God has given me my sermons, teachings and revelations about His people. It was during prayer that He revealed to me future punishment for the earth. It is in prayer that God revealed to me the death of Michael Jackson one hour before it happened. It is in prayer that God has given me countless prophetic words for the people of God, many that came to pass in that very hour. You want to know God? Do you want to experience visions and revelations? You want to be able to identify the devil from far off? Get on your knees and pray. God can't use you if He can't show you!

In prayer we wait on God and believe Him for all we need and what we don't need. When we pray we are building ourselves up in our most holy faith. Prayer builds up our faith. As we wait on God's response to our needs, our patience is being built up. Patience produces faith, the kind of faith that can weather any storm. Our belief in God and what He can do is built up over time as a result of prayer. As God answers our prayers we grow in greater trust and confidence towards Him. Waiting on God is the hard part. No one wants to wait on God for anything. Waiting takes patience and perseverance. The bible tells us that they that wait upon the Lord shall renew their strength. They shall mount up with wings as eagles; they shall run, and not be weary; and they shall walk and not faint (Isaiah 40:31). God promises that the wait will be worth it! We will be strengthened; we will run and not get tired, and we will walk and not faint.

There are several stages represented in this verse:

LET US PRAY

A.   New strength given.
B.   We will mount up-we will soar above our circumstances. We will be brought out of our problems and be given a new perspective. We will not go through the problem. We will be hoisted above our problems. Praise the Lord!
C.   We will be able to run and not get tired. Some of us will be runners in the Lord, which means we will have a new endurance in God.
D.   We will walk and not faint. Some of us will walk but not be exhausted. Anybody out there exhausted?

When we pray, we are allowing God to lead us. As we spend time in God's presence, we are creating an atmosphere for God to lead us. God cannot lead us if our heart is struggling to control everything around us. Women especially have real issues around control. We control all the management of our households, our children, the cooking; cleaning and just about everything that it takes to make our lives functional. It is because of this that we have a hard time letting God lead in our lives. Prayer helps to break down that need to control everything and make things perfect. God must lead because He is the only one who truly knows where to take you. God will not share His glory with any man or woman. Isaiah 42:8 states, "I am the Lord: that is My name: and My glory will I not give to another, neither My praise to graven images." Isaiah 48:11 b states, "and I will not give My glory unto another." God will not share His divine authority with us just to keep us happy. He does not have to. God has access to your past, present and future. He knows what is best for you. When we won't let Him lead, it is because we do

LET US PRAY

not trust Him with our lives or anything in it. Father knows best, Let God lead you because He will never steer you wrong. God knows the plans He has for you. (Jer. 29:11)

What Is It Then to Pray?

When we pray, we are being reconnected back to God on a spiritual level. Prayer can be spoken or unspoken communication to God. Meditating on God, His word or speaking to God in your mind is praying. It can be very effective because when we pray in our mind, the devil cannot hear our thoughts or concerns. The drawback is that many lack the concentration that it takes to do this and often find they drift in and out of thought so that their prayers become mindless thoughts about mundane events in their lives.

Prayer is the opportunity afforded to us to earnestly request something from God. This earnest request is a petition or supplication before the Lord (Philippians 4:6).

The word petition and supplication both mean the same thing. When we present our petitions and supplications to the Lord, we are making an appeal, we are entreating the Lord, we are making a requisition, and we are filing an application for consideration before God. These words also mean to make a plea on behalf of your own defense. When we do this, we are making an appeal to a higher authority that we acknowledge has the power to grant the request. Our supplications and petitions go before God as statements for a call to action. Our prayers should entreat the Lord and cause Him to move on our behalf.

Prayer is also an expression of faith. We cannot go to God and pray if we do not have the faith that He will respond to our cries for help. People sometimes believe that they lack the faith to pray but they get on their knees anyway and pray. Getting on one's knees and crying out to God is in itself an act of faith in a God we have not seen but trust enough to bring Him our deepest request. This is faith. Faith gets us to our knees and allows us to open our mouths and make our request known to God. It is this faith and hope in a living powerful God that allows us to ask for something that we need or want desperately from God.

Our requests to God are contained within our petitions. We make our appeal to God in the form of our applications to Him concerning all that troubles us and or all we need. In prayer we make our case and God, as the fair and just King, takes into consideration all that we have asked for and makes sure that these requests line up with His will. God will not always give us what we want but He will truly give what we each time.

To Pray Is To?

As stated before, to pray is to speak to God with faith and hope that He will listen and grant our request. The bible tells us in Hebrews 4:16 that we are to boldly come to His throne of grace. This is where we can obtain mercy and responses to our prayers. When we pray, we are to give thanks, express regret and sorrow for wrongdoing or sin (hamartia, which is to miss the mark). When we sin, we miss the mark of where God truly wants us to go. Prayer gives us the chance to cry out for forgiveness and help so that God can correct our course.

To pray is to ask for something sincerely and with passion. Prayer requires passion. Jesus in Matthew 6:7 that when we pray, we should pray without babbling and vain repetitions. In James 5:13-16, James exhorts us to pray with faith and even singing and making merry in our hearts. Prayer should be filled with passion. God is a passionate God. He gets angry (Rom. 1:18), He

LET US PRAY

rejoices (Zeph. 3:17) He grieves (II The. 2:16,17), He laughs (Ps. 2:4) He is moved from His throne on our behalf when we wait in prayer before Him (Is. 64:4) and lastly God is good to those who seek Him (Lam. 3:25).

When we pray, we are seeking to make something happen in the Spirit realm so that it can be made manifest in the natural world. Praying then is our attempt to achieve something through prayer, to make something that does not exist come into existence. Whether our prayer is for a need to be covered, or someone's chains to be broken from their lives, our prayer is trying to bring about an effect. James 5:16 tells us that the effectual prayer of a righteous man (or woman) availeth much. Our prayers should be accomplishing some kind of result. Sometimes we give up praying for someone or something because we get tired of praying for the same things. But the word of God addresses this as well. The bible encourages us not to give up but to persist in our prayer before God. In Luke 18:18 we find Jesus sharing a parable of the woman who continually comes before the judge to ask for a resolution from him concerning her enemies who were afflicting her and treating her unfairly. After much persisting day in and day out, the judge finally gives her what she needed. Persistence in prayer will bring about a resolution from God.

Prayer is worship. When we pray, we are offering up worship to the Lord. Our worship is embedded within our body posture during prayer, in our vocal praises to God, and in our acknowledgment of who God is in our life. As we pray and communicate with God we are engaging in active worship. The word worship is comprised of two words worth and ship. Worship then becomes the launching forth of the worth of God. We launch His worth through praise, worship and prayer.

In prayer we are able to exalt God. God is exalted when His children kneel down to pray. In this posture of humility, we are recognizing that He is in authority over us. We raise God's name in prayer because He is worthy of all our praise. A heart that is filled with gratitude toward God for all He has done, will not hesitate to elevate God's name. God does not need us to tell Him who He is, but we praise and exalt Him because we need to remind ourselves of who He is. The word of God is clear on this topic. Those who believe in Him and call Him their God must acknowledge God's greatness. (Ps. 147:5, I John 3:20, Ps. 48:1)

To pray is to participate in a higher level of meditation. Meditation is basically three things:
1. It is the concentration of the mind on a focused topic.
2. Meditation is the pondering of something.
3. Meditation is the serious study of a topic. Meditation is to focus on our thoughts. Our thoughts should always be connected to God. Within our thoughts we are considering God's word, His attributes and His plans for us. Meditation is deliberation. We are weighing God's way over our way. Meditation allows for contemplation. This is a deeper persistent thought on God and who He is. This is the time when we get to mentally ask those difficult questions about who and why God is? Meditation provides

time for reflection. We can reflect on all God has done, from His amazing creation down to what happens after death. Our meditation on God is encouraged through scripture. Psalm 1:2-6 tells us that a righteous man's (woman's) delight or enjoyment should be to meditate on God's law or word day and night. Doing this will cause a person to prosper and grow strong like a tree planted before deep waters before the Lord. When we meditate on God, it brings us to a state of peace or shalom (Isaiah 26:3). Shalom means more than just peace of mind, it means a complete sense of wholeness and wellness. Shalom is when everything in you is at rest and your spirit is in balance before God.

The great warrior and successor to Moses, Joshua understood how important it was to meditate on God's law. Joshua 1:8 tells us that God's law will help us observe God's word and cause us to prosper and have good (Godly) success.

The scriptures are rich with verses that encourage us and command us to meditate on God's word. Here is just a small representation of those verses (Ps. 19:4, Ps. 49:3, Ps: 119: 15, 48, 97-99, 148, Ps 104:34, Ps. 143:5, Matthew 6:6). God encourages and expects us spend time pondering on Him and His word. By doing this we can stay firm in Him; are not easily misled by false teachings; and we are given the hidden promise of being made strong so that we can be prosperous in Him! That is a great exchange.

To Pray Is Not....

We have spent a significant amount of time talking about what prayer is and inevitably the time has come to talk about what prayer is not. In order to pray effectively, we need to also know what does not work in prayer. Jesus himself warns us about what not to do in our prayer time. Matthew 6:5 "And when you pray, do not be as the hypocrites are: for they love to pray standing in the synagogues and in the corners of the streets, that they may be seen men. Verily I say to you, they have their reward." In Matthew 6:5-8 Jesus sets up the platform for what not or who to imitate in prayer.

1. Don't be like the hypocrites. A hypocrite originally was an actor playing a role or a character. Meaning they were not themselves. A hypocrite was acting out a part to be seen by others for approval or applause. We should not pray to be seen by others. I cannot pray just to please someone. Prayer must come from a heart that has had

a revelation about who God is and what He has done! We cannot pray to receive or expect praise from others. In Jesus' time, there were men who prayed on the street corners and in the synagogues loudly so that people would see them and say, "Wow" that guy is so spiritual. Look at him pray". Can you imagine someone praying on a street corner loudly just so that people will notice him or her? We need to strive to be known by God, not by others. After all, what are others going to be able to do for you or your situations? Nothing. I agree in corporate prayer and in wailing in the church together focusing on a common purpose just as long as our hearts are in the right place.

2. Prayer is not an opportunity to present a shopping list to God. We have gone through in detail what prayer is, so presenting a shopping list to God is not part of the masterpiece of prayer. God already knows what our needs are before we even ask but God wants to see us rely on Him and not ourselves. We can present our needs to God only after we have spent time in prayer acknowledging Him, thanking Him and even praying for others. My personal rule of thumb is that I leave myself for last and any personal needs I may have. I like to know that by the time I pray for myself that God's grace is ready to be poured out over me because I have demonstrated to Him that I am not the most important person on the planet.

LET US PRAY

3. Prayer is not an opportunity to blackmail God into doing things our way. This is when we tell God, in desperation I am sure, "God if you do not come through for me with this I will be forced to walk away from you, distrust you" or some other type of elaborate arm twisting. I confess that in my youth I used to try to pressure God by using some of these phrases. "God you don't love me because if you did, "-God if you don't do something about this I am just giving up on serving you" or my all-time most used phrase of all " God if you don't respond to me I will not speak under your influence prophetically or any other way again.". Even now as I write this, I am ashamed by that previous immature behavior. How dare I try to bully God in that manner? I am blessed that He did not give me a back-handed slap in the mouth. Yes, God can slap us. The bible tells us He is love but He is also a consuming fire (Hebrews 12:25), Fire burns people! Hebrews 10:31 tell us, "It is a dreadful thing to fall into the hands of God." We do not have to use forceful tactics to get God to grant our petitions. God does want us to be joyful and He wants the best for our lives. **Jeremiah 29: 11-13** reminds us, "For I know the thoughts that I think toward you, saith the Lord, thoughts of peace, and not evil, to give you an expected end (a good ending). Then shall ye call upon me, and ye shall go and pray unto me, and I will hearken unto you. And ye shall seek me, and

find me, when ye shall search for me with all your heart" (KJV),

4. Prayer is not to be used as a way to justify our sin or disobedience. Sometimes when we sin and come to the Lord to ask for forgiveness. We get the forgiveness part right but too often we also begin to justify ourselves to God. "God I am weak, I did it because you have not given me what I asked you for." Or my personal favorite "I am human and if I sin God will forgive me". Isn't this really premeditated sin? Sometimes we even blame God for our sinful slip ups. "Well God I would not have done that if you did not place that temptation in front of me." God does not tempt, James 1:13 tells us "Let no one say when he is tempted, "I am tempted by God; for God cannot be tempted by evil, and He Himself does not tempt anyone." God does try us through trials. This trying of our faith is "to see what a thing is really made of." When He tries us, He is checking to see if we are gold, silver, iron wood or hay. We are tempted by our own fleshly desires. These desires come from places of lust. Whether it is the lust of the flesh or the lust of the eyes, it is all the same. We are provided with an escape route, door, window, opening every time we face temptation. It is up to us to look for the neon sign God provides which always reads "THIS WAY OUT. Let's not ignore the sign. And by the way, don't use the devil to cover up your personal choices. I feel sometimes he gets too much credit Yes; the devil is lurking around like a

roaring Lion seeking whom he may devour (I Peter 5:8), but the verse tells us to be sober and be vigilant in the first place. Sober meaning having your wits about you. Don't flake out! Be vigilant means you are in a constant state of alertness. You are like a watchman on the wall alert and ready for the attack. The devil's success in tempting you is totally dependent on your lack of soberness and alertness. Don't make it easy for Satan to bring you down. Put up a fight! I know what you are thinking, "What about the disobedience part? Sin is disobedience. It was disobedience that led Adam and Eve to sin. Their sin ushered in rebellion into the heart of man. When we disobey, we are actually rebelling against God. Therefore, His word tells us that all disobedience is a sin unto God (I John 3:4). In Romans 5:19, Paul tells us that original sin came into the world by one man's disobedience (Adam) but that only by one Man (Jesus) could that sin be removed. Through the rebellion that was birthed in our hearts handed down through generations, our inclination is to go against God all the time. As a matter of fact, man's true nature is to sin not to live in righteousness. Our struggle is to go against the desire to sin. That is man's true desire. Only through Jesus can we live a sinless life. By this I mean a life where you are not actively looking for ways to sin against God. If we do sin however, we have an advocate in heaven to defend us, Jesus our attorney extraordinaire.

5. Be careful not to let the devil use your prayer as ammunition against you. By this I mean when we pray let's pray wisely. "God I am so tempted to steal from my job, please help me." This statement provides the enemy with leverage for future temptations against you. The devil now has information he can use against you. So, what happens is that you go to work, and he is whispering this over and over again in your ear. Then he reminds you about all the bills you have. If that doesn't work, he appeals to your pride. "Everyone else is doing better or living better than you. Are you not tired of everyone else getting ahead and you are still in the same place you were last year?" As stated before, the devil will always tempt us by using our own lusts and desires against us. A better statement to God would be "God I know you have promised to provide for all of my needs according to your riches in glory" " Philippians 4:19. This statement of prayer not only brings glory to God but it puts God in a position to honor your prayer. Our resources must always come from God. God is our supplier.

Other examples:
1. I find that married man attractive.
2. I have issues with this pride.
3. I cannot stand that person.
4. I have no desire to pray or worship God today.

Well you get the picture. All these statements can be picked up by the devil and used against you. If you have a truth statement about yourself tell God silently in your mind. The devil does not have access to our thoughts. Only God has access to the very mechanism that produces the thoughts in our head even before they are formed into thoughts (Isaiah 55:8-9).

6. Prayer is not disbelieving or distrusting God for an answer.

The bible tells us when we pray, we must pray believing that God hears us and that He will answer. In Matthew 21:21, 22 Jesus states " Verily I say unto you, if you have faith, and doubt not, ye shall not only do this which is done to the fig tree, but also if ye shall say unto this mountain, be thou removed, and be cast into the sea; it shall be done. And <u>all things</u>, whatsoever ye shall ask in prayer, believing, ye shall receive. The words disbelief and distrust are the same. Both words in the English Dictionary mean to have suspicion, misgiving, cynicism, wariness and skepticism. The word disbelieving also means to question, to refuse to accept and to have no faith. If we pray with these verbs in our spirits (verb, an action) then we are displacing (another verb, action on our part) all faith in God. Our lack of trust comes from a lack of faith. We can have suspicion because we secretly do not believe that God can and will deliver on His word and His promises.

Disbelief and distrust in what God has said or will say concerning your life, are deeply rooted in the idea that God is somehow like man and will eventually disappoint us. We become convinced that if we give God enough rope, He will let us down. When we pray, we must cast out all disbelief and distrust. The enemy uses these weapons to get us to miss out on God's blessing over our lives. God's word is crystal clear, if we believe what He has told us then those promises will be made manifest in our lives.

LET US PRAY

When we demonstrate doubt, we cancel out our faith and inadvertently delay the plan of God. Luke 1:37 tells us "For with God nothing shall be impossible." In Mark 9:23, Jesus said unto them, If thou canst believe all things are possible to him that believeth. We have a testimony if we have faith because in Romans 8:28 and we know all things work together for the good of those who love God and are called according to His purpose.

| LET US PRAY

Preparing Yourself to Pray

One prepares for prayer the way one prepares to run a marathon. You start by improving your diet, getting a good pair of running shoes, appropriate workout clothes and you begin by walking. Walking quickly helps to build up your stamina and endurance. This also helps your lungs begin to take in more air, which in turn builds endurance. Prayer is much the same way. If you are not used to praying, then you will have to build up your stamina and endurance to pray.

1. Prepare your heart for fellowship with God. When we pray, we are participating in fellowship with God. We are having a type of communion with God. Who shall ascend into the hill of Lord? Or who shall stand in His holy place? He that hath clean hands, and a pure heart, who hath not lifted up his soul unto vanity, nor sworn deceitfully. He shall receive the blessing from the Lord, and righteousness from God of His salvation",

LET US PRAY

Ps 24:3-5. The Lord requires that we come up to Him. God will not lower Himself to us again. When we come into His presence to pray, we have to come with a clean heart. We must Empty ourselves of whatever would hold us back from having intimate communion with God.

2. Confess all our sin. I John 1:8 tells us "If we say that we have no sin, we deceive ourselves, and the truth is not in us." Romans 3:23 also tells us "For we have all sinned and come short of the glory of God." We all have sin to confess to God. Whether our sin was premeditated, or we sin unconsciously, we have all sinned. Unconscious sin is when we sin unknowingly. This type of sin can occur when for example we repeat a story to someone that we have heard but the story is untrue. We however don't know the story is a lie, so we repeat it. Lying is a sin. Just by repeating a lie we lie unwillingly. Sometimes we have unconfessed sin. This is sin that we have ignored and moved on but have never really confessed it to God therefore we have not received forgiveness for it. I spoke to a woman once that despite the fact God had told her to marry someone else, she went and married a guy she wanted. She then proceeded to tell people that God gave her this man even though he was unfaithful, abusive to her and her children, attempted to leave her various times and countless other behaviors too numerous to mention. I had been telling her for years you are going

through this because of your disobedience. This woman had even made up a story about how God had brought her husband to her. It took twenty years for this woman to finally confess to me one day that this man was NOT God's will for her life. I immediately told her go confess that to God. In just one short year God started to turn her situation around. Unconfessed sin will leave you stuck for years in your miserable condition. Unconfessed sin can also be bitterness toward someone who hurt you. We cannot harbor roots of bitterness or unforgiveness towards anyone.

3. Forgive those who have hurt you (Mark 11:25-26, Hebrews 10:19). God will not forgive you if you cannot forgive others. Letting go of the right to punish someone is also known as mercy. This is what Jesus did for us; He let go of the legitimate right to condemn us and instead forgave us. When we hold on to unforgiveness we do so out of sheer pride. It is our pride that is telling us "You have every right to be angry at that person. They wronged you." When we forgive, we let go of the pride in place of mercy and compassion. If we are to be Christ-like, then we must be willing to forgive as Christ did. Bishop John Chandler Cleveland recently told me in conversation. "Forgiveness is not instantaneous. Forgiveness is a process." We must go through the process of forgiveness so that we can free ourselves from bitterness and release those who have wronged us from guilt.

LET US PRAY

4. See yourself as forgiven (Romans 6:11). We must see our sins as dead before Christ. If we have asked for forgiveness, we must accept that God is true and just to forgive us of all our sins. I believe sometimes we think it is just too easy. We ask for forgiveness and we get forgiveness. But the word of God does not lie nor does God for that matter. I John 1:9 tells us that He is faithful to forgive our sins if we confess them. It does not matter how dark our sin is, God can still forgive us. Isaiah 1:18 tells us that even if our sins are red as scarlet they will be made as white as snow. The blood of Jesus is irrevocable. Once it is dispatched on our behalf it races to cleanse us and make us new. Thank God for the blood of Jesus.

5. Have a purpose in prayer (what you are praying about or for) Matt. 7:7. When we pray, we should pray with a purpose in our heart. There are times when prayer is easier. When we are going through a trial it is much easier to pray with a focus because the focus becomes the problem. However, we can pray with focus even if we are not going through a rough time. When we pray, we can decide ahead of time what a particular prayer time will be dedicated to. Sometimes my prayer focus becomes all the women in my life that I am mentoring whether they realize that or not. There are times when my focus is my extended family. At other times my focus is my immediate family or my church family. Then there are times when my prayer becomes one of

intercession for others. It is during these encounters that God has shown me personal things about other people, their future or their past. It is also during these focused prayer encounters that God will direct me as to how to minister to someone. These are precious powerful experiences. Make your prayer purposeful.

6. Be in the Spirit (Rom. 8:26, 27) and pray with understanding (I Cor. 14:15). Praying in the Spirit means to allow the Holy Ghost to pray through you. Sometimes we do not know what to pray but the Holy Ghost intervenes and helps us pray. The Holy Ghost gives guidance especially during times of prayer when we find it hard to pray or are too broken to utter words of prayer. The Holy Spirit makes intercession for us searching our hearts and minds so that we pray according to God's perfect will. When we allow the Holy Spirit to guide our prayer then we can pray with deeper understanding because we are praying God's will into existence.

Praying in the Spirit means different things to different people. For some praying in the Spirit means praying in angelic tongues for some it does not. I do not believe that praying in the Spirit means praying in tongues all the time. Some of the most powerful Spirit led prayer times in my life were not spiritual language prayers. If I pray in tongues, I am edified but do I know what I am saying? If the Holy Ghost gives me the interpretation of what I am saying them yes, I am edified. I have prayed both

LET US PRAY

ways in tongues and not in tongues. I prefer to pray in straight English because then I know what I am saying. Don't get me wrong, there are times when I have prayed in tongues and it has been powerful and uplifting for me. But that was just for me. There is no right way to pray in the Spirit. If you are praying and you enter into a great communion with God, you can feel and hear the change in your prayer. The key point to remember is to pray with understanding.

Make sure what you are praying for is in agreement with the word of God. The Lord's Prayer reminds us to pray for God's will to be done on earth as it is in heaven. When we pray, we have to pray in agreement with God's word. We cannot pray, "God I like this married man please let him leave his wife so he can be with me." Clearly this would not be in agreement with God's word.

1. In the Ten Commandments Ex. 20 tells us "thou shall not commit adultery."
2. It also tells us not to covet anything that belongs to my neighbor. Someone could pray the aforementioned prayer, but it would not be in agreement with God's word. God WILL NOT VIOLATE HIS OWN STATUES. God will also not violate laws of nature if He does not have to. This is to say God will always choose to work in the natural first with man and then if that does not grab our attention then He moves to the supernatural (In my experience). The example here is: God will not tell a young man to marry a very old woman. Why? The law of multiplication would not occur. A union like that would not produce offspring. This example

LET US PRAY

may seem crazy but I saw a church devastated in Brooklyn, New York when a young man claimed He asked God for a wife and then said to himself, "the next woman that sits in that chair is my wife." Guess who sat in the chair? These same events were repeated in that church at least three more times. The older folk enjoyed the excitement. But in time the young men and woman that followed suit longed for children and divorced all their partners. It was a mess. Where was the observance of God's word or law in this church? Equally bad, where was the Pastor's wisdom in letting this flourish in his church?

2. Read God's word; meditate on it so that our hearts and minds can be transformed with faith (James 1:6-8). The bible tells us in James, "But let him ask in faith, not wavering. For him that wavereth is like a wave of the sea driven with the wind and tossed. For let no man think that he shall receive anything of the Lord. A double minded man is unstable in all his ways." When we pray, we must pray with faith believing that what we are praying is making its way to God's ears. Psalms 116:2 tells us that God inclines His ear to hear our prayers. What a powerful picture of a listening God. He bends His ear to hear our pleas. God is not deaf. He is also not ignoring us. But when He makes us wait for something, we have prayed for which is in His will, it builds up patience in us which in turn builds our faith. God is always working on building us up in our faith so that our hearts are transformed.

LET US PRAY

Transformed into what? Hearts that are malleable to God's voice, His will and direction. God is always working on our insides so that we walk right on the outside. The old saying is "just because someone looks good it does not mean they are good."

Examining the Lord's Prayer/Praying to God (Luke 11:1-4)

1. Our Father in heaven Holy is your name: Here we begin with the act of acknowledging God's supreme power and presence above anything else. Jesus said it is required of us to pay God our reverence and respect immediately when we begin praying. This is an act of obedience and highest worship to God. We are also called to acknowledge God's paternal role in our life. If we call ourselves His children, then we must address Him and come to Him as father. We can come to Him in reverence and still come boldly. God is our father, but He is not the guy down the. He always deserves our respect.

2. Thy Kingdom Come: We are praying for God's Kingdom to possess this world. This is no small thing. We are actually praying

for His return and for His eternal reign to take place here on earth. We are praying for the rapture. I know there are some who do not believe in the rapture however why would Jesus refer to the rapture in the Lord's Prayer. Jesus was instructing us to pray for His triumphant return to claim His church. A church without a spot or a wrinkle. (Ephesians 5:27)

3. Thy will be done: For God's will to be done on the earth should be our priority. Our desire should always be that God's will reign on earth as He reigns in heaven. In order for this to happen it starts with each individual. We must be obedient to letting God's will be done in our life. Just imagine if every Christian allowed God's will to be done in their life this earth would be in better shape. If we really mean God, then we will let him reign in our life. His will, will be our first priority in every aspect of our existence. I dare you to pray, "God make your heart's desires become my heart's desires."

4. Give us this day our daily bread: This is the place in God's prayer where we finally begin to give thanks for His constant provision. We must express gratitude for all the provision God grants us. His words tell us that if He can feed the sparrows and clothe the lily of the field, how much more significant are we ? Why sparrows because they know not where their next meal is

LET US PRAY

coming from. They don't have an owner who can feed them and protect them, but God cares for them. God must be acknowledged as the source for all our needs. God wants us to be dependent on Him and to trust Him for our provision. (Matt. 6:26-34, 10:31)

5. Forgive us our sins: If you have been reading carefully you will notice that this topic was already discussed but it is worth another look. God expects us to forgive others if we are going to need forgiveness from Him eventually. Forgiveness comes at a price which is, we must give up our right to avenge being wronged. We have to let go of bitterness and every fowl root of unforgiveness. We must practice daily the letting go of hurts and resentment. Matthew 6::15 said, "But if ye forgive not men their trespasses, neither will your Father forgive your trespasses." This is clearly stated in God's word. If we do not, forgive, we cannot expect forgiveness from God.

6. Lead us not into temptation: This portion of the prayer is a plea for help to God to help us not to fall into temptation. God cannot lead us to be tempted. The word tells us that God tempts no man, James 1:13 "let no man say when he is tempted, he was tempted by God." God tempts no man or woman. The devil tempts us using the lust of the flesh, the lust of the eyes and the pride of life. Jesus himself was tempted by Satan but He

overcame. God provides an escape when the temptation comes, I Cor. 10:13. It is up to us to take the escape hatch He makes for us. Lead us not into temptation but delivers us from evil (added in later additions) for yours is the Kingdom and the power and the glory forever and ever amen. God is capable enough to deliver us from all evil, but we must first overcome that evil by passing the temptation. Jesus was victorious not because He was tempted but because He passed every temptation the devil threw at Him. If Jesus overcame, then we can too. This is why He left such a powerful example of human self-control that can overcome spiritual wickedness.

As Promised - Constant and Consistency

In the introduction of this teaching I stated that prayer must be constant and consistent and that those two words, though they appear to be the same are somewhat different.

Constant: The word constant is an action that is ongoing. The word has numerous meanings; continuous, steady, faithful, frequent and coefficient. The word coefficient means something that is measurable or has quantity. Prayer must be measurable. We must produce prayer. In the life of a believer prayer should be measurable.

The word constant has many synonyms such as endless, relentless, persistent and perpetual. Perpetual also means effectual. The effectual fervent prayer of a righteous man availeth much (James 5:16). Our prayers must be endless and increasing so that they can bring about outcomes in our life. The word constant also means unbroken, unceasing, unremitting (not letting go) and incessant. The word incessant also means to become a pest. We must go before God to the point of becoming a pest in His presence. It was the incessant woman who day after day came before the judge to implore her case of injustice. The bible tells us that finally one day after the judge was worn down by the woman's constant imploring, he finally gave her what she needed (Luke 18:1-8). Our pray must be constant.

Consistency: The word consistency refers to behavior that demonstrates a pattern. The word consistency or consistent also has many meanings all-leading to the repetition of a pattern. The synonyms are steadiness, reliability, and uniformity (in line, patterned) evenness, stability, regularity, dependability, unswerving, and unfailing. Our prayer life should be unswerving and on track daily. Our prayer life must have a pattern; this is to say we should be praying regularly. Our heart should desire to go to God every day. I know that our lives have gotten so busy and cluttered with all kinds of activities. Praying consistently has become more and more difficult. But we can only bring our lives back into balance if we pray. Jesus asked the disciples once, "Can't you pray with me at least an hour?" The time we spend in God's presence should be enough that when we get up from prayer, we feel refreshed and renewed. We should not come out of prayer time the same way we went in. Our prayer time should provide us with enough time for us to connect with God and for God to minister to us according to what our needs are at that moment or that day.

Praying - Why Do It at All?

We have a responsibility to pray but when we pray it should not feel like a chore or a burden. Our devotion to prayer must come from our love for God and the faith we have in Him. Jesus said if you love me keep my commandments. God commands us in His word to pray. When we pray, we are actually exercising our faith. It is our faith in God that brings us to our knees time and again. If we did not have faith, we would not pray at all. Prayer is not a burden or a sacrifice. The bible tells us that God prefers obedience to our sacrifice (Hosea 6:6 and I Samuel 15:22). God wants us to obey Him because our obedience is the highest form of worship to God. When we pray, we are acknowledging Him as Lord of all.

Prayer leads us to recognize His presence with us. Prayer makes room for God to listen to our hearts. When we pray, we are talking to God and we create an atmosphere so that God can talk to us. When we pray, we become more sensitive to detecting His presence. Prayer makes us more spiritually sensitive to the move of God. Learning to understand how God is moving in our life creates a more dependent character in us. When we pray, we learn to depend more on God and less on ourselves (Col. 3:4). Human beings became rebellious once they fell into sin in the Garden of Eden. Since that time man has had a propensity towards self-reliance. Self-reliance moves us away from relying on God.

Prayer allows us to express our thanks and hope in God. When we pray, we can give God thanks for all He has done in our lives. An attitude of gratitude is extremely pleasing to God. The bible tells us that a contrite heart or a humble broken heart He will not cast out. This means God will not push us away from His presence when we come to Him with a grateful attitude. Oh, give thanks unto the Lord for He is good, and His mercy endures forever (Ps. 136:1). Everything we have and hope to have comes from Him. In God, we live and breathe. When we pray our hope in God is raised. The old gospel song said it best; "My hope is built on nothing less than Jesus' blood and righteousness; I dare not trust the sweetest frame but wholly lean on Jesus' name!" Jesus is our present hope in times of trouble. To have hope is to have an expectation that God will come through in your life. To have hope is to anticipate that God can and God will keep His promises and fulfill His plans in our live. Having hope in God is also having courage. It takes courage to believe and trust in a God we do not see. It takes courage to depend on God for all we need and want for our lives. To have hope in God is also to have faith in Him. Now faith is the substance of things

LET US PRAY

hoped for the evidence of things not yet seen, Hebrew 11:1. Can we hope enough in God to take Him at His word?

It is in God's presence that we receive the revelation of who He is and what He wants to do (Matt 7:7,8, John 16:13, Phil. 4:6,7). Matt 7:7-8 reminds us that asking of God or praying is like seeking an answer. When we pray, we are searching for a response from God. When we pray, we are searching for guidance from God for our life. Prayer is also described as a knock at a door. When we visit someone, we always ring the doorbell with the expectation that the person that invited us is home and will eventually let us in. When we visit anyone, we do so knowing that the person is home and wants us there. We do not knock with the idea that "my friend is not going to let me in." Yet when pray, we often go to that spiritual door knocking but, in our hearts, we actually believe no one is home. We knock not with an attitude of anticipation but rather with an attitude of disappointment. We expect to be let down. We ascribe human behavior to God. We think that God is going to behave like a rude person and not open the door to receive us. We cannot go to God with this preset mind. We have to go in faith knowing that God is always home and always ready to visit and chat with us for a while. Through our visit with God we obtain guidance, and, in His presence, we find peace, joy, strength and revelation. Revelation is to receive insight from God on a particular matter, idea, scripture or problem. We cannot receive revelation if we are not actively communicating with Him. Revelation comes much more easily when we are engaged in conversation with God. When God gives these revelations it brings us power, power to think, to act, behave and move forward.-Revelations 3:20 tells us "Behold I stand at the door, and knock: if any man hears my voice, and opens the door, I will come unto him, and will sup with him, and he with me."

Prayer prepares us to resist temptation (Matt 26:41) and a lack of prayer makes us weak. Prayer builds us up for the moment when temptation comes. Just before Jesus was tempted, He had walked off to pray. Jesus overcame the devil's temptations because He had strengthened himself through prayer. Yes, Jesus is the Son of God, but He was also 100% human and was accessible to fall into temptation. Every aspect of human desire, lust of flesh, lust of the heart, lust for power, and lust for fame tempted Jesus. Prayer builds us up so when temptation comes, we can, like Jesus, resist. The word resist means "to push off with great physical violence." When we resist, we are beating down the devil with great violence. If we are "prayed up" we are strong enough for the fight to resist temptation.

We need God to act in salvation towards us (II Cor. 4:4). The devil seeks to keep our minds blinded to the salvation and greatness of God. But through God's salvation we are enlightened to all of God's truths. Only God can act on our behalf to bring us to a full understanding of what He did for us and what He is yet to do.

God commands us to pray. (Col. 4:2, Luke 18:1, I Thess. 5:17, II Cor. 11:27, Matt 6:16, Luke 21:36). Simply put, God has commanded us (ordered, directed, mandated) to pray. Those of us who are parents know the frustration one feels when our child does not do what they are told. We know full well how angry and disappointed we get as parents when our children don't listen to us. God is our Father and as our Father. He gets disappointed and angry when we do not listen to Him. The most hurtful thing a child can do is to directly defy their parent. This behavior builds up frustration and can erode the relationship. To pray is to obey God's word and to also take Him at His word. God has promised to receive, listen and act on our behalf when we pray. God's actions are delayed and sometimes even abandoned on our behalf when we do not pray. Don't delay beginning a habitual prayer life today!

Types of Prayers/Prayer Can Take on Many Forms

I know what you are thinking, prayer is prayer, but that is not true. Prayer can be carried out in different ways.

1. **Worship**: When we pray, we can choose to bow down and pray. This act of bowing down is a type of worship. The Hebrew word for worship is *Shachah*. The word Shachah means to bow down from the waist, to prostrate oneself to the ground. When we pray sometimes, we are compelled to humble ourselves and bow down. The act of bowing down is an act of worship itself. God sees this physical action of bowing down as worship. "If my people who are called by my name would humble themselves and seek my face then I would…" Our worship, as stated before, has to be done in spirit and in truth (John 4:23), which is to say, our worship must be done in spirit (in the and through the spirit of God

i.e., the HOLY Ghost) and in truth. In truth means in the knowledge of who God is. God is the truth. Jesus is the truth, the life, and the way. No man comes to the Father but by Him (John 14:6). Truth is obtaining the sincerity of mind and integrity of character, which comes when we know Jesus. Truth must come from that inner part of us, our heart that receives the revelation of God Ps 5:11. When we Shachah we are surrendering our heart to the Lord. This surrender comes from an expression of love and admiration for God. This is a spiritual response from the Holy Ghost who reveals to us who God is. Shachah is a voluntary submission to the will of God and to His statutes. God does not want to twist your arm to get us to recognize who He is in prayer. That can only come through revelation. A full revelation of God brings about an outburst of deep praise and worship. When we worship God in this way, we set ourselves up to hear His voice. This alone is glorious and to be sought after.

2. **Confession:** Prayer can be confession. When we pray, we can confess our sins and failures to God. This provides us with the opportunity to seek God's forgiveness for our life. We should always confess what the word tells us about sin. The wages of sin is death (Romans 6:23, Is. 3:9, Prov. 11:19). Sin enslaves the participant (Rom. 6:22, 6:16). Sin separates us from God (Is. 59:2). Sin creates a gap between us and God. This is why Jesus had to come and reconcile man

LET US PRAY

back to God. Jesus and the cross create a bridge from us back to God. Our verbal confessions express faith in God and His word. When we verbally recite God's word back to Him, we are releasing God's blessing on ourselves. If we believe in our heart and confess with our mouth that Jesus is Lord, we will be saved. All who call on the Lord will be saved (Rom. 10:13, Acts 2:21, Joel 2:32, I Cor. 1:2). To call on the name of the Lord is to acknowledge Him as Lord and to acknowledge that only He can forgive us of our sins.

3. **Thanksgiving:** When we pray, we are expressing thanksgiving to God. Offering thanksgiving is another form of praying. When we give thanks, we are communicating appreciation for the Lord. We are to give all our gratitude to the Lord. The declaration of our thankfulness is encouraged in the scriptures (Ps 18:49, Ps 136:1-3, Ps 107:1, Ps 106:1, Ps 92:1, II Sam. 22:50, I Chron. 16:8, I Chron. 16:34). We are to thank God for blessings seen and unseen. All good things come from the Lord (I The. 5:18). A grateful heart will find a way to give God thanks. When we do not thank God then we are being ungrateful. The word tells us to give thanks unto the Lord for He is good, and His mercy endures forever. A heart filled with gratitude becomes easily overwhelmed when it ponders all that God has done on our behalf.

LET US PRAY

4. **Praise:** Praise includes everything we can use to make a joyful noise unto the Lord. This includes all types of praise, singing, music, words, shouting, clapping, dancing, loud and soft praise are considered prayer before the Lord. The playing of instruments, the use of our voice to shout to the Lord is also praise. People who are not completely free in God will experience a great deal of trouble praising God with liberty. Sometimes people do not feel comfortable displaying outward praise to God in public, but the bible tells us if we are ashamed of Him here then He will be ashamed of us in heaven (Matt 10:32, Mark 8:38). We cannot be ashamed to display our love for the Lord. Our praise is an outward display of affection. PDA, Please Display Affection to God. He loves it. There is also a spiritual release that comes with our display of public praise. God releases and deposits joy into our spirit when we worship Him. This release of joy brings strength to our life (Neh. 8:10, Ps 28:7).

5. **Petition:** Our petitions should always be in line with what God's will is for our life. Sometimes we ask for things that are not in God's plan for our life. When we make our own choices even if they are well meaning, we may still end up suffering the consequences of those choices. I often meet with people that are suffering and when I begin to go over the story of their life, I ALWAYS find the link back to where they let go of God's hand and took up their own

direction. I have seen people suffer divorce, their child taken from them, abuse, financial hardship, sickness, and mental illness. So many of these events can be completely avoided. People who are leading themselves through life often blame God the minute they find themselves suffering these hardships. The problem is, God had nothing to do with it. Sometimes many of these hardships are connected to the person we marry or the people we let into our life. We are drawn away from God's will by the lust of the flesh, eyes and heart. These desires lead us to have clouded judgment where we ignore clear signs that a person is no good for us. I also know people who marry someone because they are lonely. However, the loneliness is then saddled with additional problems. I cannot stress enough how important it is to make sure that God is directing our life choices (Pro. 3:6, Ps. 37:23,24, Ps 37:4,5, James 1:5). When God is our Lord then He can direct us. Listening to God's direction can make or break your life (Is. 30:21). I married my husband because a) God spoke to my entire family in a service I had not attended, b) God gave me love for him, c) I have seen and enjoyed a life with my husband that has been absolutely amazing! There is nothing better for us than to enjoy God's gifts to us via His choice and not ours. There is no comparison. A good life is okay, but an excellent life is better! (Ps 40:5, Is. 53:6, Is 14:24, Is 14:24, Is. 55:8,9, Jer. 29:11)

6. **Intercession:** Prayer is making intercession for and on the behalf of another. The word intercession itself means interceding, attempting to resolve conflict and prayer or petition. When we intercede through prayer for someone, we are trying to resolve a conflict on behalf of someone else. To be able to intercede we truly have to be able to feel that person's pain or be able to put oneself in the position of another. We can experience brokenness on behalf of a loved one, relative friend or sister/brother in Christ. When we intercede for another, we are standing in the gap for someone. In prayer we bring the needs of others before the Lord. I have often told people, "If you worry and take care of others instead of only concerning yourself with your needs, you will force God to take care of you." God is very concerned about intercession. In I Tim. 2:5-6, we are exhorted to intercede for all men through our prayers and supplications. Jesus was sent to the earth to make the greatest intercession of all, to die for all men and serve as a mediator between God and man forever (II Tim. 2:5-6, Rom. 8:34). Jesus also told us that He would send the Comforter who in turn would make intercession on our behalf as well (Rom 8:26, Rom 8:27). If we have all this intercession being made for us, then we must be able to offer up that intercession on behalf of someone else.

7. **Waiting:** Waiting on God to answer and trusting Him with the answer are the two

most difficult areas for Christians. For some people waiting is the most difficult thing of all. Ps 27:14 tells us that if we wait on the Lord our heart will be strengthened. This simply means that our faith will be made strong when we wait. This may not make sense to anyone. If I wait my heart and faith will be made strong? When we wait, we are required to exercise patience and patience produces faith. Most people think that if God gives us everything right away it would make us more faithful, not true. Just like children, our anticipation grows when we wait. Children wait for Christmas all year long, but their faith is not shaken instead they get more excited the closer Christmas gets. When we wait on Christmas or on Christ, with us grows the excitement of the fulfillment of God's promises over us. Waiting is just the gap between the time when the promise is made and the time when the promise is made manifest. Waiting is not forever; it is just a pause. When we wait on the Lord, we are pausing to give God a chance to speak to us. Waiting also means stillness, to have peace of mind, heart and spirit. Waiting is a quiet active stillness in God. Waiting in God's presence can bring powerful breakthroughs, revelations and creative ideas flowing. Don't be afraid to wait on the Lord.

8. **Warfare:** Spiritual warfare is a very real type of prayer. When we are warring in prayer, we are using the word of God to tear down the powers of darkness (Ps 149:6-9).

LET US PRAY

Ephesians 6:11-12 says, "Put on the whole armor of God, that ye may be able to stand against the wiles of the devil. For we wrestle not against flesh and blood, but against principalities, against rulers of the darkness of this world; against spiritual wickedness in high places." There is a process we must follow if we are to be effective at-waging war against the enemy.

a. We must be fully dressed in God's armor; Eph. 6:13-17.
b. Then we must be able to resist the wiles of the devil. This means we cannot engage in sin, fall into temptation and then think we have power against the devil. It is not happening.
c. We must then resist which is to fight with great violence against the enemy.
d. Know God's word well. Our prayer, praise and God's word are weapons that directly impact the powers of darkness (fallen angels). During the warfare prayer, we can pronounce judgment against these fallen angels. We can command them to leave their positions or post of influence and authority in the name of Jesus to clear the way for a move of God (Matt. 16:19, Mark 16:17). I was praying during the summer of 2013 and I was led by the Spirit to pray for the spiritual dryness here in the Tampa Florida area. As I prayed for God's refreshing and this dryness to leave, I began to ask God to show me why this area had been so spiritually dry for so many decades. As I prayed, I had a vision. I saw a map of this entire region and a huge glass dome lid over

the entire area. On top of that huge dome there was a huge demon. But this was no ordinary demon. I could see that he was high ranking. He had a black uniform on with bars on his shoulders. He also had a huge spear that was even taller than he was. I yelled out to God "who is that?" and immediately the Lord said, "this is the principality in charge of this small region. He is the one that has been keeping back the spiritual rain from falling in this area. He has been keeping back revival." I began to weep. Lord what do I do? The Lord said you have power to take him down, use it. I began rebuking that demon, cursing him back to hell, deposing him from his position. I prayed with an authority that frightened even me! Afterward I felt a sense of relief because I know that his reign in this area had come to an end. When we are living for the Lord, prayed up and know how to use our spiritual gifts, then God can call on us to take the enemy down. Warfare prayer can also be used to command sickness to leave in the name of Jesus. We can call for healing over someone and they will be healed. This is one of the reasons Jesus came, to give mankind power over his enemy (I John 3:8 and Acts 10:38). The bible reminds us that we have been given power to tread upon snakes and scorpions and nothing would hurt us (Luke 10:19). This verse is not to be taken literally, but it is a spiritual description of the authority God has given His children over the enemy. We do not have to cower in fear of the dark, witches' spells, voodoo,

Santeria, spiritualism or black magic. There is so much that I can say about spiritual warfare because it is a huge topic in the Christian world. I do recommend that everyone read at least one book on spiritual warfare. I strongly recommend "Thou Shall Expel Them "by Derek Prince and "Pigs in the Parlor" by Fred Hammond and Ida Mae Hammond. The first book I read on spiritual warfare was Rebecca Brown's first book on this topic Prepare for War and He Came to Set the Captives Free; it changed how I prayed when it came to the enemy. Again, dealing with the casting out of demons and tearing the enemies high place is not for people who are not living right or who don't have a strong prayer life. I also believe that some people are truly called and gifted with a special anointing to deal with the enemy. This is not for the faint of heart or the wishy-washy.

9. **Praying in Tongues:** Praying in tongues is sometimes called praying in the Spirit. I prefer to call it praying with the Spirit. As I stated before you can pray in the Spirit and not speak tongues. Simply put, praying in the spirit is allowing the Holy Ghost to; a) lead the direction of your prayer, b) who the Holy Ghost directs you to pray for, and c) praying with anointing and power. There are times when while you are praying, the presence of God is so strong it causes you to speak in tongues. This happens to me at times. When I am praying and begin to speak in tongues I listen carefully because there are times when I can interpret my own

tongues. This does not happen to me often, but it has happened on occasion. This usually means to me that God is saying something that He does not want understood by others around me. When we pray in tongues only God and sometimes the person understands what is being said. As I said before I prefer to pray in Spanish or English because I completely know what I am saying to God. Praying in tongues is very edifying to the person who is using their tongues. Through the speaking of tongues, we connect to God on another level and it also brings a lot of comfort and joy to the person. I Corinthians 14:2 tells us that speaking in tongues allows us to speak to God and through this experience we speak mysteries. The book of Jude, verse 20, tells us that speaking in tongues builds us up spiritually. People believe that those who speak in tongues do not have a sense of what is going on around them. This couldn't be farther from the truth. When we speak in tongues, we are participating a higher spiritual level and actually become more aware and sensitive spiritually. Our minds are completely engaged in the experience. Our mind is not going blank or dark but quite the opposite. Speaking in tongues has been studied and is still being studied by scientists.[22] When you pray or meditate in a mindful state, your brain produces alpha and theta waves consistent with serenity and happiness, allowing your harried thoughts to have a reprieve. Prayer and meditation can cause a generalized reduction in multiple physiological and biochemical markers, resulting in decreased heart and respiration rate, decreased plasma cortisol (a major stress hormone), decreased pulse rate, and increased EEG (electroencephalogram). Groundbreaking research is revealing that these disciplines can also literally reconfigure the brain's biology, triggering biochemical and neurological changes that are therapeutic. This reconfiguring can make a big difference in one's health and well-being. Just as scientists have found that positive beliefs can engender wellness (the placebo effect), they also have found that negative beliefs and influences can induce illness (the "nocebo" effect) Debra Furham, PhD - Health Care. The medical community has also found that people who pray in tongues experience the same effect on the brain that drug users experience when they get high on drugs. The same areas that light up when a person is high on drugs are the same areas that light up in the brain when people pray in tongues. There are great breakthroughs connected with the praying in tongues. It is a gift available to all who have received the Lord into their hearts as their Savior. The bible tells us it is a gift promised from God for His children (Acts 2 and Mark 16:15-18). We must believe and ask God for this gift.

10. **Group Prayer:** Recently I received a call at 5:53 am from a young woman who had been hospitalized the day before for a routine fibroid removal. The day before she went to

the hospital, we spoke, and I encouraged her. I could hear in her voice that she was going through a crisis of faith and that she was afraid of what was going to happen. What I did not know was she was questioning everything the Lord had been saying to her for the last year or so. So, when I received the call from her at 5:53 am I was not surprised. She immediately told me that she was bleeding internally and that the doctors told her if the bleeding did not stop, they would have to remove her uterus. This young woman received a word from the Lord telling her, "she would marry and have two children." I quickly told her "No, this is not going to happen." I began to pray a prayer of belief in the promises God had for her. You will live and see the promises of the Lord come to pass in your life. When I told my husband he quickly responded with "it's time to pray." We both prayed for her again. I laid in bed worrying and questioning God. Isn't that what the devil wants us to do? To question God's already stated promises, to get us to doubt what He has declared over your life? As I questioned God as to why this was happening, I heard the voice of God clearly say to me, "This time next year she will be with child," Lydia does not worry. I have this. God's voice and clear decision made me smile and then laugh. In this state of peace, I fell asleep. When I woke up again, I started to activate a group of women who I know will pray no matter where they are. I had women in Florida and Massachusetts praying for the

LET US PRAY

young woman. My message to them all was "this is a 911 call"; I need you to pray that the enemy will not have the victory over this woman's life. It would be another seventeen hours before I would get the news that the doctors were able to stop the bleeding and her uterus was saved. It would take another day before I could speak to her. I told her that she had been through her own Gethsemane Garden. It was in the garden that Jesus won the victory over the cross. It was in His moment of extreme sorrow that Jesus surrendered His will for that of His Father. When Jesus went into the garden, He went in crying on His face but when He left the garden He left saying "Let us arise the hour is at hand." This word arises means to be resurrected. Jesus was saying I have been resurrected to God ~~and already~~ and I will advance towards the enemy; I will not run from Him. I will confront the enemy because I know what the will of the Father is, and His will, will be done. Why have I shared this story with you? There are times when we need to come together and pray. When we come together in a group agreeing on one thing God will respond. The bible tells us in Matthew 18:19 that if any two would agree on one thing on earth it would come to pass. There is a great power that is released when we agree in prayer for anything. God shows up when He sees and hears this gang of faith praying together. When we can gang up on a problem or an issue on behalf of someone, we are creating a wall of spiritual warfare that God cannot ignore. God responds to the prayers of His people. I must at this point say however that we must know whom we are asking to come into agreement with us in prayer. The people we invite to come into prayer with us must be people who know how to intercede for others. They must be able to put themselves in the shoes of another person. They must also be people who are actually going to pray. When I made the 911 calls for prayer, the women ended up praying around the clock, so that the young woman was covered in prayer throughout the day and evening. That's what I call a wall of warriors. Do you have a wall of warriors you can count on? If you don't, start thinking about a warrior wall of your own that you can call on during times of trouble.

Summary

At the beginning of this study I invited the reader to go on a journey to discover what prayer is and why it is so important to God that His children pray. The Kings James Version of the bible mentions prayer 114 times. To pray is mentioned 313 times. Prayed is mentioned 65 times and praying is mentioned 20 times. Altogether God speaks to us about prayer 512 times in His word. There are 650 different prayers listed in the bible. God brings our attention to the act of praying 1,162 times. This is why this topic is so important to the Christian community.

We cannot call ourselves God's people and then at the same time abstain from spending time in His divine presence. God is a God of relationship. God is seeking and will continue to seek a relationship with His people but not forever. The bible tells us that the Spirit of God will not contend with man forever. Gen. 6:3 and Is. 57:16 reminds us of this fact. The word contend, deserves a closer look. The word contend in the English dictionary means to struggle against, to compete with and to argue with. This means when we resist going into God's presence our spirit is in a struggle with God. We are competing with God to see who will win this battle. When we are engaging in contention with God, we are arguing with Him. Let's just make one thing clear, that is an argument you are going to lose every time. The word contends has several synonyms; resist (to fight with violence), oppose, deal with and put up with. God will not put up with our foolishness forever.

LET US PRAY

The word contend in Hebrew has additional meanings. In Hebrew the word contend is the word *rib* or *rub*. Here the word is a verb or action word. When we **rob** God or rob Him, we are poking at Him with a stick, we are rubbing against Him in the wrong way. God is a consuming fire; we should not want to rub against Him at all. The words *rib* or *rub* also mean to dispute, find fault with, have a quarrel with, judge, and plead a person's case and reprimand. When we *rub* or *ruob* God, we are finding fault with what He is directing us to do. We are reprimanding God about what He has instructed us to do. It is like a child correcting his own father when his father tells him to "clean your room". The word contends has an even deeper meaning in Arabic, which is the closest language to Aramaic, which is the language Jesus spoke. The word contends in Arabic means to agitate the mind, to disquiet the mind. When we contend with God, we are frustrating the mind of God. Another way to look at it is that we are disturbing the peace of God or frustrating His grace towards us. We are destroying our own favor before God when we agitate Him about our responsibility to pray. The word contend in Syriac also means to cry out loud, to shout, to clamor and quarrel loudly. When we ignore God in prayer, we are shouting out to Him that we don't have the time to talk to Him, we are dismissing Him like we dismiss people we are fed up with. Be careful! God loves us but He will not put up with our disrespect or disobedience.

Make a prayer plan today. Stop resisting God and ignoring His word. Get back into God's good graces, pray!

The Prayer Appendix

To get you started on a prayerful road, I would like to share some helpful prayers that you can pray over different members of your family. I have used these prayers and have shared them with others who have seen God change, deliver, save and restore those around them.

Praying for Your Husband

What does the bible say about prayer?
1. We should pray daily Ps 55:17 "Every evening, morning, and at noon time, will I pray, and cry aloud: and He shall hear my voice" Ps5: 3.
2. Pray in secret and God will respond openly to Matt 6:6.
3. When we have trouble getting the words out in prayer, the Spirit prays through us Rom. 8:26.
4. Be diligent in praying especially when things are not going well Rom. 12:12.
5. Pray with confidence and faith that God is listening to Phil. 4:6.
6. Pray without ceasing I The. 5:17.
7. Pray wherever you can without anger and doubt I Tim. 2:8.
8. Pray when you're sick or afflicted James 5:13.
9. Pray for others and you will be healed (made whole) James 5:16.
10. Pray for those who hurt you Matt 5:44.

LET US PRAY

Why should I pray for Him?
1. Praying for your husband is like praying for yourself. Genesis 2:24 "For you and your husband are one flesh."
2. Your family and children are blessed through your prayer.

What do I pray over my Husband?
1. Pray for his spiritual growth and maturity (gifts and their development).
2. Pray for God to give him wisdom to make good decisions.
3. Pray for him to be a man shaped in the image of God (fruits of the spirit Gal.5:22-23).
4. Pray for his ministry and purpose in God.
5. Pray that God makes him an excellent father, teacher and mentor to your children.
6. Pray that he be an understanding, loving, thoughtful and considerate husband.
7. Pray that he understands your needs and responds to them.
8. Pray that he be a good lover, tender and gentle.
9. Pray for his good health, physical and mental protection.
10. Pray for his work environment to be positive and not stressful.
11. Pray that God creates opportunities for advancement at his job.
12. Pray for his financial prowess.
13. Pray for him not to fall during times of temptation.
14. Pray for his daily safety:

LET US PRAY

15. Pray that he always serves and loves God.

You thought you did not have a whole lot to pray about, didn't you? Think again.

Ten Things to Pray for Our Children

James 5:16 reminds us that the effectual fervent prayer of a righteous man avails much. This word avails means to accomplish. When we pray fervently, which means always, our prayer will accomplish a great deal in the lives of those we pray for.
How are we praying for our children? Are we leaving their futures up to chance?

1. **Pray for Godly wisdom**: (I Cor. 3:19, Romans 12:2, James 1:5) Ask for God to give your children wisdom to make good Godly choices.
2. **For Character**: This is hard because our character is built through trials. Your children are no different. (Romans 5:3,4) This is a process that produces a strong future. Ask for a healthy dose of self-control to come over their lives. Pray that as a mother you can stay out of God's way of what He wants for your children.
3. **For a Spirit of Excellence**: (Daniel 6:3, I Cor. 10:31) Pray that your children will give of their best to everything they do. Let them know they represent Christ on this earth and what they do has His name on it.
4. **For Humility**: (Gal. 5:22-26) The world admires pride, arrogance and self-righteousness. Pray that your children

understand God admires humility. (James 4:6, Matt 23:12). Pray that your children understand their worth comes from God and He expects them to walk in meekness.

5. **For A Desire to Know God**: Pray that your children have a deeper walk with God and a real personal relationship with God. (Ezra 8:22, Ps 86:11) Pray they have a hunger and thirst for God and an individual heart to seek and serve Him with abandonment. God must be taught to take first place in our children's hearts.

6. **For Direction**: (Prov. 3:5-6, Eph. 2:10) Pray that at a young age they would seek God's guidance and direction before they make serious decisions. For example, career, college and marriage. If you teach this, they will be in the habit of following God's perfect will every step of their way in their life. (I started praying for my children's companions since they were born. By the age of 8 and 6 God had already spoken to me through a prophet's mouth that God had already chosen their wives. I cannot tell you what a relief this was for me. Since then (now they are 27 & 25) God has confirmed this word three more times. I am at rest and at peace about their mates. This praying thing works!

7. **For Favor in God**: The book of Esther is a book that demonstrates the favor of God on a child who obeyed God and her guardian. The favor of God was on Esther and the King chose her to be Queen. This one decision saved an entire nation. (Luke 2:52) Pray that your children have the favor of

LET US PRAY

God in their lives. That they are favored by everyone and wherever they go. That they also appreciate the gifts and talents God has given them.

8. **Discernment** (I Kings 3:5) Solomon was given a chance by God to ask for anything he wanted but he chose to ask for wisdom. Pray that your children have spiritual sight to see as God sees for their lives. That they are attracted to what God is pleased with and that they reproach what God reproaches. Ask that God give them insight to know God's will for their lives and that they see it clearly and consistently.

9. **For the right friends/Spouse:** Abraham prayed for God to give Isaac a wife and the servant prayed to God for the sign for the right young woman. God came through for Abraham, Isaac and the servant. Pray that your children marry believers of the faith. Pray that their in-laws be saved, and that God would be in the center of their relationships forever. (II Cor. 6:14) Pray that God gives them Godly friendships that will encourage them and not lead them away from God. Who our children spend time with and marry can make or break their future, destroy their lives and cause them to lose their purpose in God and can even determine where they end up in eternity.

10. **Respect toward Authority:** Children are taught by everything in their surroundings not to fear or respect their parents or those in authority over them. Yet the bible directs us in Rom. 13:1 that we must have reverence or respect for those in authority or rule over us.

LET US PRAY

Pray that your children would have the proper respect for their parents and even their future bosses. Pray that they have appropriate respect and fear of God (the beginning of wisdom is the fear (or reverence) of God Prov. 1:7, Prov. 9:10, Ps. 11:10.

If you have not been praying for your children, then start today. It is never too late to pray for your children Phil. 4:6.

A Teenagers/Young Adults Prayer

This list came to me about five years ago. I shared with a woman at my gym and she used it as a platform of spiritual discussion with her three daughters about prayer. It changed how her daughters prayed. Currently all three young women are experiencing God's grace and the oldest is set to marry this August. Prayer works! This is just a short list to help your teenager or young adult pray and focus on the things that are important before God for their lives.

1. Give thanks to the Lord for everything He has given you.
2. Clothes, food, shelter, health and a sound mind.
3. Give God praise for His grace and favor. For all the doors He has opened and will open for you.

LET US PRAY

4. Lord forgive me for all my sins. Wash me in your blood don't let me sin.
5. Lord thank you for guidance, please continue to guide me.
6. Lord give me wisdom to make good decisions and to use good judgment.
7. Lord give me the desire to serve you and worship you with freedom.
8. Fill me with your Holy Spirit Lord I need it.
9. Draw me closer to you now more than ever before.
10. Lord surround me with people who love you and can be supportive of me.
11. Lord remove anything and anyone who would try to hinder me from my purpose in you.
12. I know Lord you have a plan for my life, please let me realize that plan in my life.
13. Lord give me self-control help me to be disciplined.
14. Lord bless my parents and give them wisdom as they guide me.
15. Help me to keep my heart, mind and ears open to your advice and that of my parents.
16. Oh Mighty Lord provide for the daily needs of my family and me.
17. Lord let me help others and not overlook other's needs.
18. Lord place your gifts in me and help me to allow you to use me.
19. Lord cleanse my heart and give me a spirit of excellence.
20. Lord bless my extended family (give my grandparents health and provision.
21. Lord set my uncles and aunts free to be who you want them to be.

22. Lord keep my cousins safe and help them to love and serve you.
23. Protect all my relatives and fulfill your word in them.
24. Lord increase your wisdom and fruits of the spirit in me.
25. Lord help me to be the woman/man you need me to be.
26. Lord make me a great son/daughter, friend and in the future a great spouse.
27. Lord let me love you and follow you and your word all the days of my life.
28. Lord help me to be faithful and obedient to you all the days of my life.
29. Lord let your light shine in me and through me.
30. Lord I praise you now and always Amen.

My Family's Personal Prayer List

This prayer list that I am sharing with you has been our family's personal list for years. My husband of 32 years and I update it as our lives change and situations develop that need more or less of our prayer time. We also pray together once a week. I whole-heartedly recommend this for all couples in our Covenant Marriage Ministry because it promotes intimacy and it moves God to action. The bible tells us that if any two would agree on one thing on earth it will be done (Matt 18:19, Jesus speaking). Take the time to read it and draft a prayer list with your husband and see what God can accomplish as a result of your obedience and unity.

LET US PRAY

PRAYER LIST

- PRAISE GOD
    - Let us bow down and worship You. (Ps. 95:6 & 99:5)
    - Let us worship You and serve You only. (Mat. 4:10 & Luke 4:8)

- LOVE GOD
    - Help us love You with all our heart, all our soul, and all our mind. (Mat. 22:37, Mark 12:30, and Luke 10:27)
    - Let us fear You, follow all Your ways, hold fast to You, serve You with all our heart and soul, and keep Your commandments. (Dt. 10:12-13 & 11:22)
    - Help us to love others as You have loved us. (John 13:34)

- **THANK GOD**
    - Salvation
    - Your love and sacrifice
    - Your mercy and forgiveness
    - Your promise
    - Your word and its guidance in our life

- The opportunity to serve You and others
- Those who pray for us
- Pastors and brothers and sisters who provide spiritual support
- Spouse
- Children
- Home
- Providing for our needs
- Work
- Health
- Keeping us by You

- **SET OUR PRIORITIES**
  - Help us to set our hearts on Your kingdom first and go on Your saving justice. (Mat. 6:32)
  - Let us give You our first fruits as You keep Your promise to us. (Gen. 28:20-22)

- **GOD'S PROMISE**
  - Your word is greater than your name. (Ps. 138:2b)
  - Your word says that those who ask to receive. (Mat. 7:8)

LET US PRAY

- Your word says that if we have faith, we will receive everything we ask in prayer. (Mat. 21:22)

- Your word says that if two of us agree to ask anything at all, You will grant it. (Mat. 18:19)

- Your word says that you know what we need before we ask it. (Mat. 6:8)

- Your word says that when we do not know how to pray the right way the Spirit will make our petitions in a way that cannot be put into words. (Rom. 8:26)

- **SPIRITUAL MATTERS**

  - Give us a spirit of repentance. (Mat. 4:17)

  - Let us be unassuming. (Mat. 5:4)

  - Let us desire uprightness and justice. (Mat. 5:6)

  - Let us be merciful and forgiving. (Mat. 5:7 & 6:14)

  - Let us be pure in heart. (Mat. 5:8)

  - Let us be peacemakers. (Mat. 5:9)

  - Let our good works be seen so that You may be praised. (Mat. 5:16)

LET US PRAY

- Help us speak clearly. (Mat 5:37)
- Help us be givers. (Mat. 5:42 & 6:3-4)
- Help us love our enemies. (Mat. 5:44)
- Help us pray. (Mat. 6:6)
- Help us fast. (Mat. 6:18)
- Help us focus on heavenly treasures. (Mat. 6:20)
- Let us serve You and not money. (Mat. 6:24)
- Let us trust in You. (Mat. 6:27-27)
- Help us not to judge. (Mat. 7:1)
- Let us not make the profane the sacred the sacred (Mat.7:6)
- Help us stay on the straight and narrow road. (Mat. 7:14)
- Give us a spirit of discernment. (Mat. 7:15-20)
- Help us hear Your voice and act on it. (Mat. 7:21-27)
- Let us speak with a voice of authority. (Mat. 7:29)
- Give us faith in Your power. (Mat. 8:13)

LET US PRAY

- Help us stay true to You. (Mat. 12:30)
- Help us control our words. (Mat. 12:37)
- Help us to not ask for signs. (Mat. 12:39)
- Help us do your will. (Mat. 12:50)
- Help us see and hear Your will. (Mat. 13:13)
- Help us think as You and not as men. (Mat. 16:23)
- Give us a spirit of service. (Mat. 20:28)
- Give us wisdom.
- Let us revere You always.
- Make us purposeful.
- Make us consistent and disciplined.

- **FORGIVENESS**
  - Forgive our sins and cast them into a sea of forgetfulness.
  - Forgive our limited trust.
  - Forgive us for falling short.
  - Forgive us for not serving You with all we have.

LET US PRAY

- Forgive us for not being the perfect spouse, parent, friend, or colleague.

- Let our prayers for forgiveness be a constant reminder and spiritual conviction of what we must change, and we pray that You make those changes in us all.

- **PRAYER FOR YOUR PEOPLE**

    - Let us see—in response to their prayers or otherwise—that You are our God and that we are Your people.

    - Let us see that You confer a special benefit unto us.

    - Let us see that Your word is true and is even exalted above Your name.

    - Let us see that You are the God of the living.

    - Let us always recognize that You are worthy to be praised and glorified.

    - Share in Your abundance and meet our needs in all aspects of our lives.

    - Guide us and lead us to Your perfect purpose.

- **CHURCH**

    - Make us a church that pursues You above all things.

LET US PRAY

- Put in us a spirit of selflessness that makes you the priority in our lives and convict us to replace our thoughts with yours.

- Develop and mold us in our spirit, in our hearts, and in our minds so that we can serve You and serve others as You meant it to be.

- Make us a church of love and communion.

- Make this a church where your spirit moves freely—with confidence and without constraint.

- Make this a church where the gifts of the spirit are manifested among us all.

- Make this a church that impacts Your community, Your Nation, and your globe.

- Give us wisdom in all things.

- Make us desire greater prayer and worship.

- Make ~~our us~~ our hearts willing to give of our time and resources.

- Give us hearts that seek justice and fair dealing.

- Make us effective in our ministries.

LET US PRAY

- Protect and bless Your people, the leadership and the visitor so that we may never forget that You are the Lord, that You are good, and that You supply our needs.

- Make us supporters of Your word, those who spread it, and those who work for Your goodwill.

- Bless us in this facility and any other facility You may have for us.

- Above all things let us never forget You, as Your people have done so often, instead let it be said that we have been faithful to You and pleasant in Your sight.

Epilogue

When I started to put this piece of writing together, I did not know that it was going to be so long. I do not apologize for the length of this study nor do I call this an extensive study on prayer. I believe I have barely scratched the surface of what prayer is. I did however receive a prophetic word twelve years ago where God told me "Pick up your pen and begin to write again. You used to write all the time and I have gifted you to do this" Out of fear and self-doubt I did not do what God told me. Then again three years ago another prophet of God came to my church and again told me," Pick up your pen." I will pour out books and volumes of books that are in you. People will expect you to write about what you know, education and children. But God has books for women and men in you, God has shown me that you will even write children's stories that you made up for your boys when they were little that are completely original, with characters you made up for your children when regular children's books did not satisfy them. You will write books that sinners and saints will want to read. Get to write my daughter."

I have written this study, as an introduction to what I know will be a lifetime of books for God's people. Please take the time to read through it but not all at once. You can even use this study as a devotional for your personal prayer time. The important thing is that you take the time to read it not because it will make me happy but because I

LET US PRAY

know it will bless you as this has come out of a long road of obedience for me. I have also prayed that as you read this study God will minister to you and convict, bless and lead you in how and when He needs you to pray. At no other time in our country's history has there been a greater need for God's people to pray. "Remember if my people who are called by My name would humble themselves and pray and seek My face and turn from their wicked ways, then I will hear from heaven, and will forgive their sin and heal their land (II Chron. 7:14)

If you take one thing away from the reading of this study let it be this, "It's time to pray!

Thank You

I have often said that a person is only as good as the people that surround them. Putting this book together did not happen by itself nor did I do all of this by myself. I thank God for the revelation, motivation and inspiration to write this book. Without my God I cannot do anything at all. My God is too good to me.

I want to thank my husband for being so kind to me during the days and nights I did not talk or spend time with him because I was busy writing.

I also want to thank Bishop John Cleveland for writing the forward or preface for this, my first book. I only notified him days before all final drafts. Thank you, John.

Finally, finally, but not least I want to thank Jai-Lin Gray for editing this piece of work for me and taking this body of work to its finished look. You know what you mean to me but now so does everyone else.

A special thank you to Emily Velez for taking this book and translating it into Spanish for all my Latin Sisters of the faith. Te amo.

About the Author

Lydia E. Rivera Torres was born and raised in Brooklyn, New York by her Parents Rev. Jesus M. Rivera and Angelina Rivera alongside her two sisters and two brothers. God called Lydia Torres at the ripe age of five when God filled her with the Holy Spirit during an all-night watch service at the International Revival Tabernacle in Brooklyn. That moment brought with it the voice of God, and a prophetic anointing, which increased in Lydia with every passing year.

The Lord opened the door for Lydia to attend college on a Scholarship and she was able to graduate with Honors from Bernard Baruch College with a Bachelor's Degree in Early Childhood Education in 1984. A Master's Degree in Elementary Education followed in 1988 with another Master's Degree in Educational Administration and Supervision in 1992. These educational advances led to an educational career that included 11 years as a classroom teacher and as an alternative learning styles specialist as well as seven, and 7 years as an Assistant Principal and Principal. Lydia is currently looking forward to enrolling in graduate school to seek a PhD in Organizational Management.

In 1986 God brought Christopher Torres into Lydia's life and they were married in 1988. In 1992 God's miracle healing brought a first son Christopher Llorens Torres after four miscarriages. Their second son, Xavier Sebastian Torres followed in 1994 as God decided to show off one more time.

LET US PRAY

Lydia and Chris have been called into ministry and have successfully created five different ministries that are still blessing others. Individually, Lydia and Chris have served in over eight ministries and are still sought after for advice in ministry development. Lydia and Chris started working with married couples over 14 years ago; this ministry work led to the establishment of the Covenant Marriage Ministry in 2003 and the development of an extensive teaching manual. This ministry has opened the door for marriage conferences, marriage classes, and couples counseling throughout the United States.

In 2011 Lydia and Chris became ordained ministers through the Global Impact Ministry. Lydia has been preaching throughout the United States since she was ten years old and has seen God work healings, miracles and deliver individuals from sinful addictions. In last four years Lydia has been ministering to women of all ages and is currently the founder of Esther's Court Ministry which focuses on the empowering of all women to become who and what God intended them to be.

On September 29, 2013 Lydia and Chris opened up the Restoring Life Ministry Church in Riverview Florida. This assignment from God was the fulfillment of a prophetic word they we received ten years ago. The Lord worked on both our hearts until they we surrendered to His will. God is currently is blessing them us with energetic devoted people that are looking to impact their community for the Lord.

Lydia and Chris are looking forward to God's continued grace in their lives knowing that

LET US PRAY

their submission and obedience to His will is all He wants from them. Amen.

www.ingramcontent.com/pod-product-compliance
Lightning Source LLC
Chambersburg PA
CBHW032022040426
42448CB00006B/698